My
Little House
Sewing Book

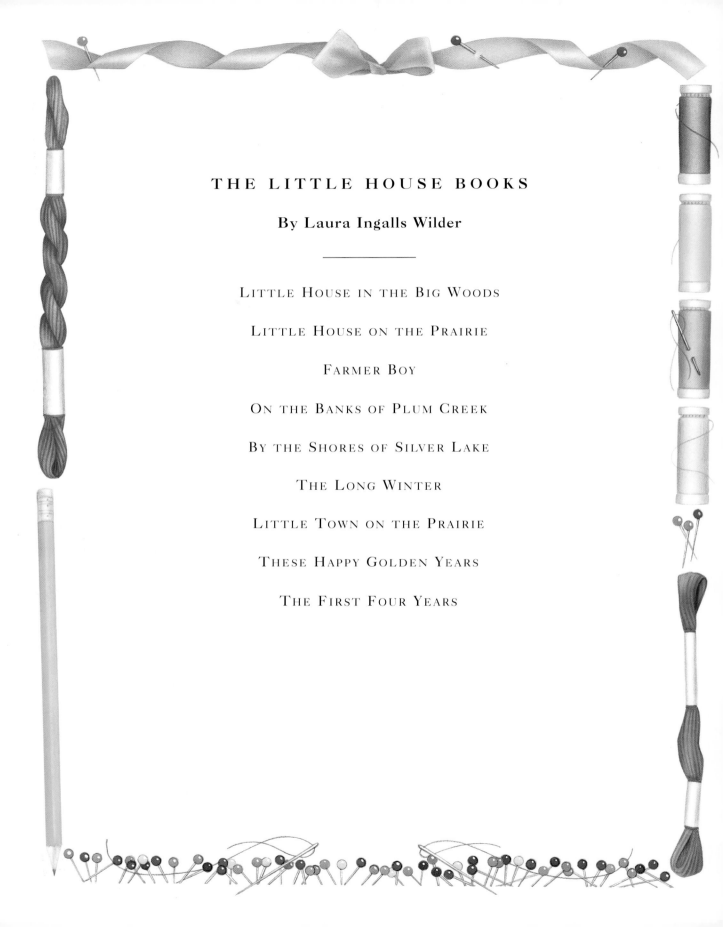

THE LITTLE HOUSE BOOKS

By Laura Ingalls Wilder

LITTLE HOUSE IN THE BIG WOODS

LITTLE HOUSE ON THE PRAIRIE

FARMER BOY

ON THE BANKS OF PLUM CREEK

BY THE SHORES OF SILVER LAKE

THE LONG WINTER

LITTLE TOWN ON THE PRAIRIE

THESE HAPPY GOLDEN YEARS

THE FIRST FOUR YEARS

LITTLE HOUSE

Laura Ingalls Wilder

My Little House Sewing Book

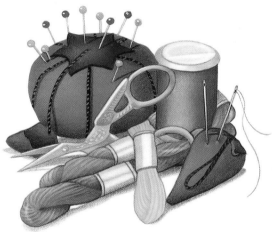

8 Projects from
Laura Ingalls Wilder's Classic Stories

BY *Margaret Irwin*

ILLUSTRATED BY *Mary Collier*

HarperFestival®
A Division of HarperCollinsPublishers

LITTLE HOUSE
Laura Ingalls Wilder

To Tim, Meghan, and Parker

and to my Mother

who taught me how to sew

—M. I.

To my little sewers,

E. K. and E. C.

—M. C.

My Little House Sewing Book
Text copyright © 1997 by Margaret Irwin
Illustrations copyright © 1997 by Mary Collier

Quotations taken from the following Little House books by Laura Ingalls Wilder: Little House in the Big Woods, *text copyright 1932, copyright renewed 1959, Roger Lea MacBride;* Little House on the Prairie, *text copyright 1935, copyright renewed 1963, Roger Lea MacBride;* Farmer Boy, *text copyright 1933, copyright renewed 1961, Roger Lea MacBride;* On the Banks of Plum Creek, *text copyright 1937, copyright renewed 1965, Roger Lea MacBride;* By the Shores of Silver Lake, *text copyright 1939, copyright renewed 1967, Roger Lea MacBride;* The Long Winter, *text copyright 1940, copyright renewed 1968, Roger Lea MacBride;* Little Town on the Prairie, *text copyright 1941, copyright renewed 1969, Roger Lea MacBride.*

HarperCollins®, ®, HarperFestival®, and
Little House® are trademarks of HarperCollins Publishers Inc.
Printed in Hong Kong.
Typography by Alicia Mikles

Contents

Full-sized patterns can be found in the pattern pocket at the back of the book

Introduction

IN THE LITTLE HOUSE BOOKS, Laura Ingalls Wilder tells the story of her life with her family on the American frontier. Laura and her family moved many times, lived in many different houses, and often were far away from any town or neighbor. Laura grew up in an era without modern conveniences like electricity, indoor plumbing, or refrigeration, when all the family members, including Laura and her sisters, had to work together to grow their own food, build their own houses, and even sew their own clothes. Everyday life then was very different than it is for us today.

Because ready-made clothing was expensive and often not available on the frontier, sewing was a skill necessary for survival. Ma made all the clothing for her family and, like all pioneer women, taught her daughters, Mary, Laura, Carrie, and Grace, how to sew. Many pioneer girls learned to stitch on fabric scraps, often sewing something useful, such as a quilt. All the seams on a patchwork quilt are short and straight, making it easy to learn on. In *Little House in the Big Woods*, Laura was just five when she began to make a patchwork quilt. In the other Little House books, Laura describes making many hand-sewn items, including an apron for Ma, a necktie for Pa, clothes for Carrie's and Grace's dolls, and her own wedding dress. She even took a job sewing shirts to help raise money to send Mary to college in *Little Town on the Prairie*.

Sewing was necessary to make many everyday household items, such as bedsheets, quilts, curtains, and rugs. Pioneer women also sewed many crafts, toys, and gifts for their homes, families, and friends. Although so much sewing meant a lot of work for pioneer women, it also provided a pleasant opportunity for them to visit with other women, and to exchange patterns and ideas.

The sewing projects in *My Little House Sewing Book* have been selected from the Little House books for you to sample the different kinds of sewing that pioneer girls and women did. Today, both girls and boys will enjoy sewing these projects. They are arranged from the easiest to the most difficult, so you can make the projects in order and learn as you sew each item. There are eight projects in all: the needlebook Ma made for Aunt Eliza in *Little House in the Big Woods*, Laura's nine-patch pillow from *Little House on the Prairie*, the handkerchief Carrie made for Mary in *Little Town on the Prairie*, Mary's braided rug and Laura's embroidered picture frame from *The Long Winter*, Alice's embroidery sampler from *Farmer Boy*, Laura's doll apron from *On the Banks of Plum Creek*, and the sunbonnet Laura wore in *By the Shores of Silver Lake*.

The **Sewing Supplies** section lists the things you will need to make the projects. Many sewing supplies are much the same today as they were in Laura's day. To sew, you still need fabric, scissors, needle and thread, just as Laura did. Some of the projects in this book also require supplies Laura did not have; they will help you to make these projects more easily than Laura could have. Laura and her family loved the "new-fashioned" ways of their time and were eager to try any new method that would make sewing go more quickly. In *These Happy Golden Years*, Laura tells how delighted Ma was when Pa surprised her with a new sewing machine!

The **Sewing Skills** section tells you how to sew the basic stitches you will need to make the projects in the book. More stitches are listed in the *Stitch Guide* on p. 39. Read through the **Sewing Skills** section carefully before you begin a project, and use it as a guide if you need help. You may even want to practice each of the stitches and skills on scrap fabric before you begin a project. Laura had to practice making stitches when she learned to sew, too!

All the projects in this book can be made by a beginning sewer. However, you may need some help from an adult to learn how to follow sewing directions. Before you begin to make a project, be careful to read the directions completely, so you know exactly what materials you will need and what you will need to do. Each project has a list of supplies you need so that you can choose the fabric and colors of thread or embroidery floss that you like. Remember: Anytime you need to use an iron, you should always ask an adult to help you.

Finally, to make the projects as simple as possible, there are full-sized printed patterns included in the pattern pocket in the back of the book. Just find the patterns you need for each project and cut them out. After you use a pattern, put it back in the pocket for safekeeping, until you want to use it again.

My Little House Sewing Book will help you to learn to sew, just as Laura did, so you can make some of the same things Laura herself made. Take your time, and enjoy each step. Learning to sew by hand allows you to experience the ways of long ago and to develop a skill that you can enjoy today. Happy sewing!

In the whole store there was nothing but dry goods. Laura had never before seen a store where nothing was sold but dry goods. At her right hand was a short counter-top of glass, and inside it were cards of all kinds of buttons, and papers of needles and pins. On the counter beside it, a rack was full of spools of thread of every color.

LITTLE TOWN ON THE PRAIRIE

 # Sewing Supplies

Thread: Use white quilting thread. It is strong, easy to thread, and doesn't tangle easily.

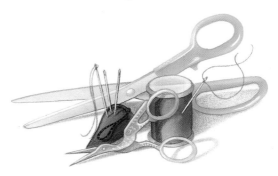

Needles: Use sharps, size 7 or 8, for hand sewing. For sewing with embroidery floss, use embroidery needles, size 7 or 8, which have a larger eye (hole). A #22 tapestry needle is used with yarn or floss on perforated paper.

Scissors: Use a pair of scissors with 3½-inch blades for cutting fabric. Smaller scissors, often called embroidery scissors, are helpful for snipping sewing threads.

Fabric: Has a right and a wrong side. The right side is brighter and shows the design most clearly.

Pins: To hold fabric in place while you sew. Pins with round plastic heads are easy to pull out of fabric and easy to see if you drop them.

Pincushion: To keep pins and needles safe when you are not using them.

Pencil: Use a sharpened pencil to mark the sewing and cutting lines on fabric. On dark fabrics, use a white or a light-colored pencil. Never use a marker on fabric, as it might not wash out.

Ruler: For drawing straight lines and measuring.

Poster board: Very stiff paper sold in stationery supply stores.

Embroidery floss: This has six threads, twisted together, which can be separated.

Transfer pencil: A special wax pencil used to transfer an embroidery pattern onto fabric. Keep the pencil tip sharp for best results. You can buy a transfer pencil in a craft or fabric store.

Perforated paper: Stiff paper with holes in it for stitching.

Stuffing: Polyester fiberfill is sold in fabric and craft stores. One 12-ounce bag will be enough to fill the nine-patch pillow.

Glue: Use white glue or a glue stick for fabrics and paper. A glue stick is less messy.

Mary was still sewing nine-patch blocks.
Now Laura started a bear's-track quilt. It was harder than a
nine-patch, because there were bias seams, very hard to make smooth.
Every seam must be exactly right before Ma would let her
make another, and often Laura worked several days on one short seam.
ON THE BANKS OF PLUM CREEK

Sewing Skills

Marking fabric: For some projects, you will be marking your fabric by drawing a sewing line and a cutting line. Always draw lines or other pattern marks on the wrong side of the fabric, unless the directions tell you to draw on the right side.

Cutting fabric: Cut fabric on a large table or on the bare floor. Follow the cutting line, and keep the fabric flat. Make sure your scissors are sharp enough to cut fabric easily. Be careful not to scratch the surface you are working on!

Pinning: Place the two pieces of fabric to be joined right sides together. Pin the layers at one end of the marked sewing lines. Pin at the other end of the marked lines and every two inches along the lines. Make sure the sewing lines on both pieces of fabric match. When you are sewing, remove the pins as you come to them.

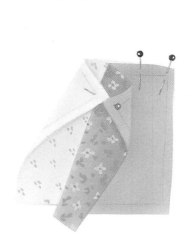

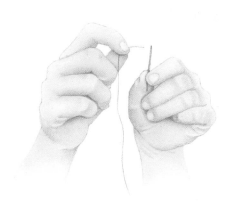

Threading a needle: Cut a piece of thread about 18 inches long. Hold the thread close to one end, and push this end through the eye of the needle. If you have trouble threading the needle, or if the end of the thread starts to fray, re-cut or lick the end of the thread and try again. To help thread yarn through a needle, fold a small narrow rectangular piece of paper in half over the yarn end; or you can buy a needle threader in a craft or fabric store.

Beginning knot: Thread a needle. Take the end of the longer strand, and cross it over itself to form a circle. Fold the end under the thread, and bring it up through the loop. Pull tightly on the end to form a knot. Cut the thread, leaving a ¼-inch tail.

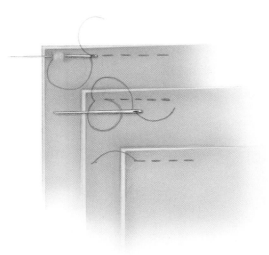

Ending knot: When you have finished stitching, go back and make a stitch over your last stitch. Do not pull this backstitch tight, but pull only until a loose loop of thread is left. Guide the needle through this loop; then pull the thread tight. Take another backstitch over the first one to hold the knot tightly in place. Cut the thread, leaving a ¼-inch tail. When sewing with embroidery floss, make a stitch under the back of your last stitch, instead of into the fabric.

Sewing: To make stitches with a needle and thread. Right-handed sewers work from right to left, and left-handed sewers work from left to right. Left-handed sewers can turn the diagrams upside down to make them face the same direction they will be sewing.

Running stitch: This stitch looks like a dotted line. Thread a needle, and make a beginning knot. Bring the needle up through the fabric at the beginning of your sewing line, and pull until the knot catches on the under-side. Move the needle forward $\frac{1}{8}$ inch  along the sewing line, and push it back through the fabric. While the needle is still in the fabric, push the needle tip forward another $\frac{1}{8}$ inch along the underside of the fabric. Then bring the needle tip back to the surface of the fabric to form a stitch. Pull the thread through; then begin the next stitch. Check the underside often to make sure you are sewing on that line, too. Try to make your stitches small and all the same size.

Backstitch: This stitch looks like a solid line. Thread a needle, and make a beginning knot. Bring the needle up through the fabric on the sewing line, $\frac{1}{8}$ inch away from the beginning of the sewing line, and pull until the knot catches on the underside. Put the needle into the fabric $\frac{1}{8}$ inch away from where the thread has just come 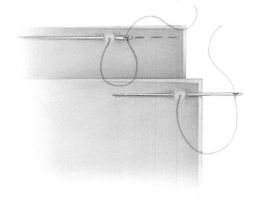 through, at the beginning of the sewing line. Now push the needle tip along the underside of the fabric, past the knot, and bring the tip back up to the surface, farther along the sewing line, $\frac{1}{8}$ inch away from where the thread last came through. For the next stitch, go back to the end of the last stitch to put the needle through the fabric and come up a stitch length (⅛ inch) ahead. Continue to make stitches by going back with the needle to connect the line and then coming up ahead.

Whipstitch: This stitch wraps over two folded edges of fabric to join them together. Thread a needle, and make a beginning knot. Pin the two fabrics to be joined with their edges folded together on the inside. Hide the beginning knot by placing the needle between the two folded edges and pushing the needle up through one fold until the knot catches inside the fold. Push the needle through the fold of the other fabric, and pull until the stitch is tight. Continue making small, even stitches through the folds of both layers of fabric by always pushing the needle into the fabric from the same side. When you come to the end, make an ending knot. To hide the thread tail: Push the needle back into the fold of the fabric at the knot, bring the needle tip back to the fabric surface ½ inch away from the knot, pull the thread through, and cut the thread close to the fabric.

Clipping: When a sewn seam is curved, it must be clipped in order to lie flat. Make several small cuts, ¼ inch apart, from the edge of the fabric toward the sewing line. Do not cut through the line of stitching.

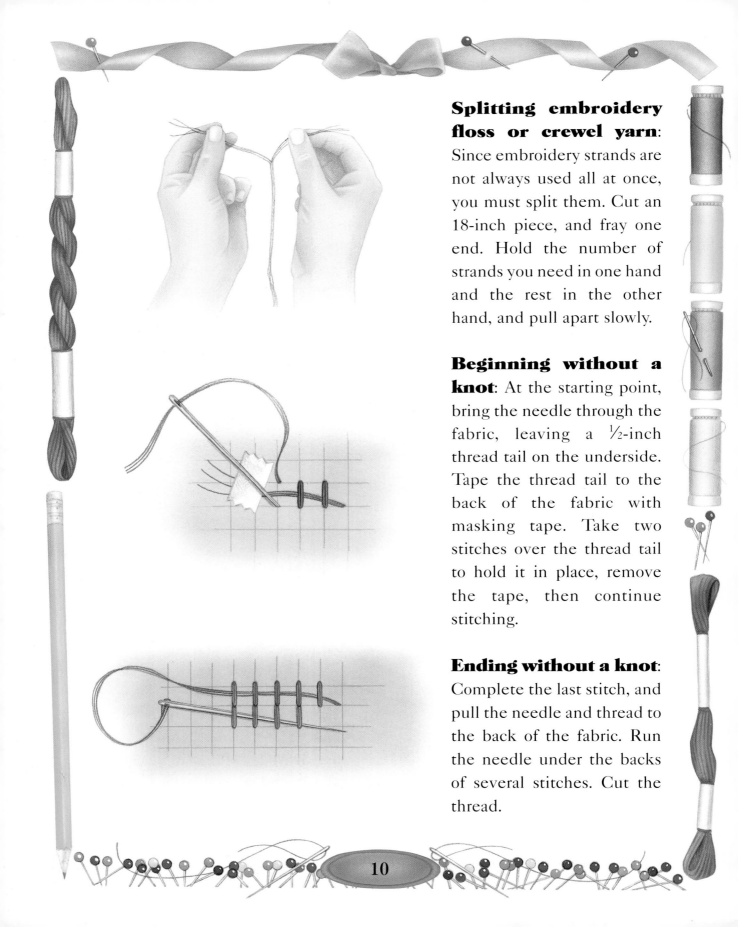

Splitting embroidery floss or crewel yarn: Since embroidery strands are not always used all at once, you must split them. Cut an 18-inch piece, and fray one end. Hold the number of strands you need in one hand and the rest in the other hand, and pull apart slowly.

Beginning without a knot: At the starting point, bring the needle through the fabric, leaving a ½-inch thread tail on the underside. Tape the thread tail to the back of the fabric with masking tape. Take two stitches over the thread tail to hold it in place, remove the tape, then continue stitching.

Ending without a knot: Complete the last stitch, and pull the needle and thread to the back of the fabric. Run the needle under the backs of several stitches. Cut the thread.

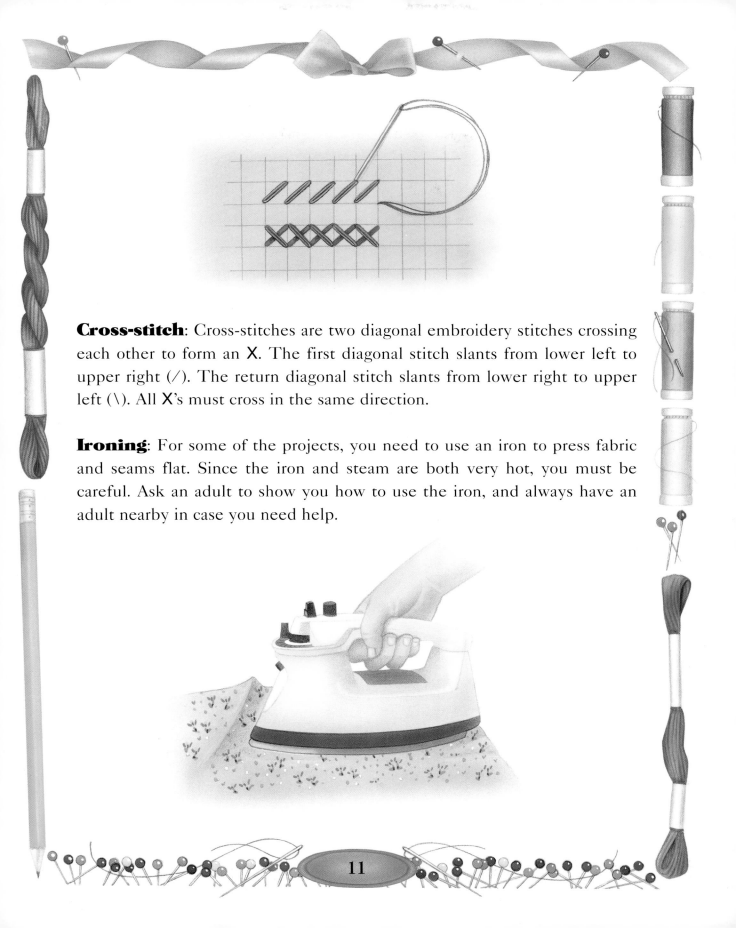

Cross-stitch: Cross-stitches are two diagonal embroidery stitches crossing each other to form an **X**. The first diagonal stitch slants from lower left to upper right (/). The return diagonal stitch slants from lower right to upper left (\). All **X**'s must cross in the same direction.

Ironing: For some of the projects, you need to use an iron to press fabric and seams flat. Since the iron and steam are both very hot, you must be careful. Ask an adult to show you how to use the iron, and always have an adult nearby in case you need help.

Ma gave Aunt Eliza a little needle-book she had made,
with bits of silk for covers and soft white flannel leaves into which to stick
the needles. The flannel would keep the needles from rusting.
LITTLE HOUSE IN THE BIG WOODS

 # Ma's Needlebook

Laura's Aunt Eliza, who was Ma's sister, her husband, Uncle Peter, who was Pa's brother, and their children came to spend Christmas with Laura and her family in the Big Woods of Wisconsin. Ma's gift to Aunt Eliza was a hand-made needlebook for keeping her needles safe. In return, Aunt Eliza gave Ma a large red apple stuck full of cloves. "How good it smelled!" thought Laura.

You will need:

4 x 6 inch piece of satin or calico
*   fabric*
4 x 6 inch piece of white flannel
½ yard of ¼-inch-wide ribbon
scissors
poster board
white paper
embroidery floss

needle (embroidery)
pins
ruler
pencil
masking tape
glue or glue stick
Heart Pattern from the pattern
*   pocket*

1. On your satin or calico fabric, use your ruler and pencil to draw a rectangle that measures 5¼ x 3½ inches. Cut out this rectangle of fabric, and fold the 5¼-inch side in half like a book. Crease the fold with your thumbnail. Unfold, and place the fabric, wrong side up, on a flat surface. With a ruler and a pencil, draw a line ⅛ inch from the center fold on each side.

2. Cut out two rectangles of poster board, each measuring 2 x 2½ inches. Spread a thin coat of glue on one side of each rectangle. Place each rectangle, glue side down, on the wrong side of the fabric. Make sure each piece has one long edge on each line you drew on the fabric. There should be ¼ inch between the two pieces at the center fold and ½ inch of fabric outside the other three edges.

3. Put a dot of glue on each of the four outside corners of the poster board, and fold the fabric over the poster board to form triangles at the corners.

4. Put a thin line of glue along each of the three outside edges of each piece of poster board. Do not put glue along the center edges, since you will not be putting fabric there. Fold the fabric over the poster board along the top, bottom, and side edges, to glue in place.

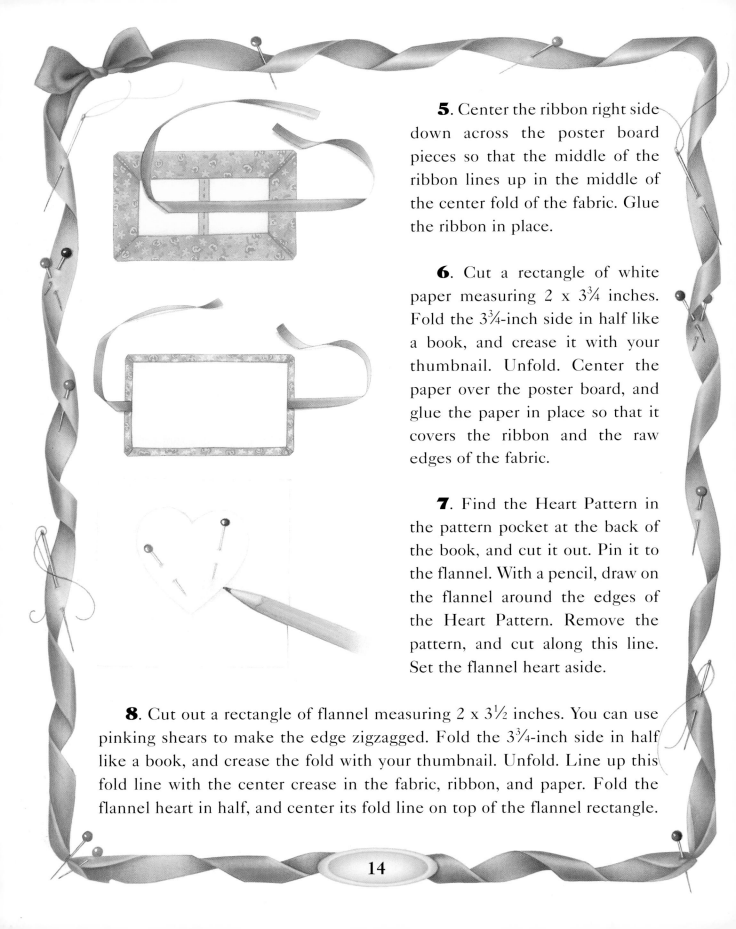

5. Center the ribbon right side down across the poster board pieces so that the middle of the ribbon lines up in the middle of the center fold of the fabric. Glue the ribbon in place.

6. Cut a rectangle of white paper measuring 2 x 3¾ inches. Fold the 3¾-inch side in half like a book, and crease it with your thumbnail. Unfold. Center the paper over the poster board, and glue the paper in place so that it covers the ribbon and the raw edges of the fabric.

7. Find the Heart Pattern in the pattern pocket at the back of the book, and cut it out. Pin it to the flannel. With a pencil, draw on the flannel around the edges of the Heart Pattern. Remove the pattern, and cut along this line. Set the flannel heart aside.

8. Cut out a rectangle of flannel measuring 2 x 3½ inches. You can use pinking shears to make the edge zigzagged. Fold the 3¾-inch side in half like a book, and crease the fold with your thumbnail. Unfold. Line up this fold line with the center crease in the fabric, ribbon, and paper. Fold the flannel heart in half, and center its fold line on top of the flannel rectangle.

Hold the two flannel pieces in place on the paper by placing masking tape over the edges.

9. Cut an 18-inch piece of embroidery floss. Split the floss to two sections of three strands each. Thread the needle with one three-strand piece, and tie a beginning knot. Carefully lift the edge of the paper at the center fold line. Push the needle up through the paper close to the edge to hide the beginning knot under it. Make a backstitch over the edge of the paper. With a running stitch, sew through the layers of the flannel, paper, and fabric along the center line. Make an ending knot. Guide the needle under the top layer of fabric, close to the knot, and bring the needle tip up ¼ inch away. Cut the floss close to the fabric surface. This will hide the floss end.

10. Fold your needlebook, and tie the ribbon in a bow to close. Push needles (and pins, if you like) through the flannel leaves of the needlebook for safe-keeping.

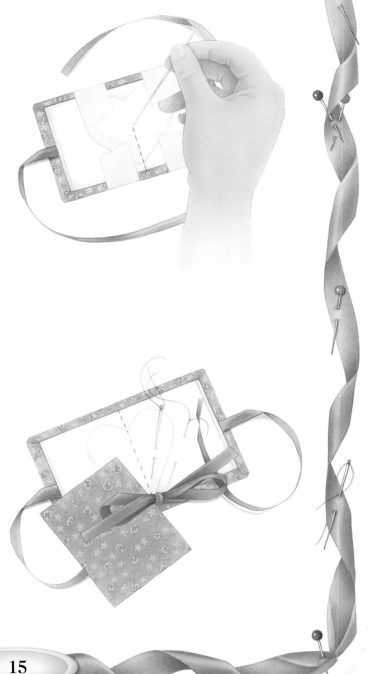

The days were short and cold, the wind whistled sharply,
but there was no snow. Cold rains were falling. Day after day the rain fell,
pattering on the roof and pouring from the eaves. Mary and Laura
stayed close by the fire, sewing their nine-patch quilt blocks.
LITTLE HOUSE ON THE PRAIRIE

 # Laura's Nine-Patch Pillow

The winter Laura spent in Indian Territory in Kansas was long and cold. On rainy days Mary and Laura stayed inside with Ma, learning how to sew by stitching the short, straight seams of their quilt blocks.

You will need:

½ yard main calico fabric (any	*pencil*
small-patterned cotton)	*pins*
¼ yard second calico fabric	*ruler*
thread	*stuffing*
needle (sharps)	*4-inch Square and 4½-inch Square*
scissors	*Patterns from the pattern pocket*

1. Find the 4½-inch Square Pattern in the pattern pocket, and cut it out. Lay your ½-yard piece of fabric, wrong side up, on a large flat surface. Pin the pattern to the fabric as shown in the layout guide.

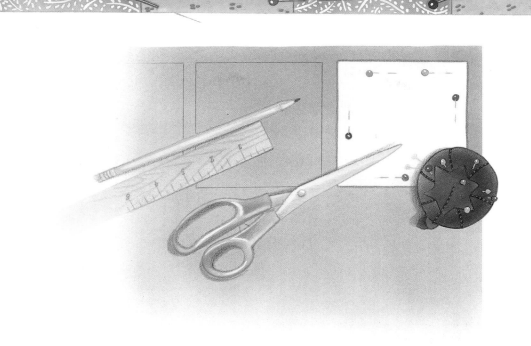

2. With a pencil, draw around the edges of your pattern to mark the cutting line on the fabric. Remove the pattern. Use this pattern to mark four more squares on this fabric, and four squares on the second fabric. Mark the squares close together, to save fabric for the back of pillow. Cut out the squares following the lines. You now have nine patches.

3. Find the 4-inch Square Pattern in the pattern pocket, and cut it out. Pin it to the wrong side of one of the cut squares, $\frac{1}{4}$ inch in from all four edges. With a pencil, draw around the edges of the pattern to mark the sewing line on the fabric. Remove the pattern, and repeat this step on the other eight squares.

4. With a ruler and a pencil, mark a 12-inch-square sewing line on the wrong side of the main fabric. Draw a cutting line ¼ inch outside the sewing line, by first measuring and then making a mark about every inch all the way around the square. With a ruler and a pencil, draw a line connecting all the marks. This new outer square is your cutting line. Cut out the square following this line. This is the back of your pillow.

5. Take one 4½-inch patch of each color, and place them right sides together. Pin the squares together along one side edge, matching the sewing lines. Thread a needle, and make a beginning knot. Start sewing at one corner of the square. With a running stitch, sew along the sewing line. Make your stitches as small and even as possible, and remove the pins as you sew. Check both pieces often to make sure your stitches are on the sewing lines. Sew to the end of the line, and make an ending knot. Do not turn the corner!

6. Pin a third patch to your strip. Make sure to alternate colors by joining squares of different fabrics together. Sew, following Step 5. You now have one complete strip.

7. Sew two more strips with your remaining patches, following Steps 5 and 6. Make sure the patches alternate up and down *and* side by side when you lay the strips next to each other.

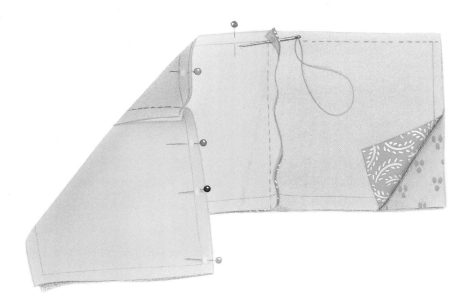

8. Pin two strips, right sides together, matching the corners of each of the squares along the seam. Thread a needle, and make a beginning knot. Begin at one end of the sewing line, and sew with a running stitch. As you sew across the first patch, you will come to the cross-seams. These are seams, already sewn, that you must cross over, and not stitch into, as you sew a new seam. Hold both cross-seam allowances ahead of your stitching, out of the way, and sew to the corner of the square. Push the needle through the layers of one cross-seam allowance; then move and hold both cross-seam allowances behind your stitching, out of the way, as you continue stitching on the next square. Do not sew the cross-seam allowances flat in your seam. Repeat at each cross-seam. Make an ending knot when you reach the end of the seam.

9. Pin and sew the third strip to your six-patch block to complete the nine-patch block.

10. Place the nine-patch block, right side down, on an ironing board. Use an iron set on "cotton/steam" to press each seam flat toward the darker-colored fabric, so that it won't show through to the right side. Do not open up the seam. Flip the block over, and lightly press on the right side, making sure the seams are flat against the darker-colored fabric.

11. Pin the nine-patch block and the pillow back right sides together. Make sure the corners and the sewing lines match up. Thread a needle, and make a beginning knot. With a running stitch, starting at one cross-seam, sew along the sewing line. Make sure your stitches are small and even so the stuffing can't come out. Remove the pins as you sew. Sew the entire seam on three sides. On the fourth side, stop sewing at the other cross-seam, in order to leave a four-inch opening. Knot your thread securely with an ending knot.

12. Turn your pillow right side out through the opening. You can use the corner of a ruler or the eraser end of a pencil to push out the corners. Fill the pillow with stuffing.

13. Fold the fabric on the sewing lines on both sides of the pillow opening so that the extra fabric is inside the opening. Pin the folded edges together. Thread a needle, and make a beginning knot. Sew the gap closed with a whipstitch. Make an ending knot.

The Christmas box had gone to Mary. In it Ma carefully
placed . . . the lace collar that she had knitted of finest white sewing
thread. Then she put in six handkerchiefs that Carrie
had made of thin lawn. Three were edged with narrow,
machine-made lace, and three were plainly hemmed.
LITTLE TOWN ON THE PRAIRIE

Carrie's Lace-Edged Handkerchief

When Mary was at the school for the blind in Iowa, it was too expensive for her to return to Dakota Territory to spend Christmas with her family. So Pa, Ma, Laura, and Carrie carefully packed a Christmas box filled with their presents, including Carrie's handkerchiefs, a long letter, and a five-dollar bill. Christmas would not be the same without Mary, but when Mary received the box she would know that her family was thinking of her.

You will need:

⅜ yard of any white cotton fabric   *needle (sharps)*
    (lawn is very delicate and sheer   *pins*
    fabric)   *scissors*
1½ yards of ¾-inch-wide white   *ruler*
    ruffled lace trim   *pencil*
white thread

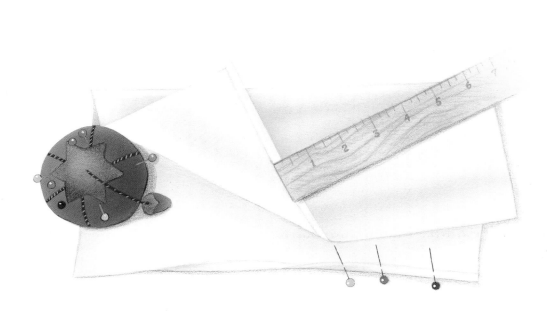

1. Lay out your fabric, right side down, on a flat surface. With a ruler and a pencil, measure and mark a 12-inch square. Cut out the fabric square on the marked line. Place the fabric square, right side down, on an ironing board. Fold one edge over about ¼ inch toward the wrong side. Use an iron set on "cotton/steam" to press the fold. Repeat this step on the other three sides.

2. Fold over the folded edge another ¼ inch, and press with the iron as in Step 1. Pin the double-folded hem in place. Repeat this step on the other three sides, making sure the corners are neatly folded. Lay your fabric square, right side down, on a flat surface. You are now ready to pin on the lace.

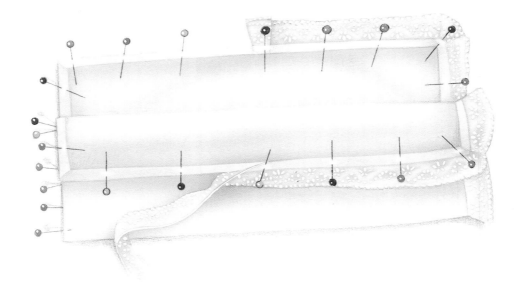

3. The lace has a ruffled edge and a flat edge, and it has a right side and a wrong side. On the wrong side, the stitching is not as pretty and even as it is on the right side. Fold one cut end of the lace back ½ inch to the wrong side, and pin. Beginning at the center of one side of the fabric square, place the right side of the folded end of the lace on the wrong side of the fabric. Pin the flat edge of the lace to the double-folded edge of the fabric, so that the ruffled edge is outside the fabric square. After you have pinned them, check that the right sides of both the fabric and lace are on the other side.

4. Pin the lace to the double-folded edge of the fabric every inch along the sides. When you reach each corner, fold the lace to match the corner of the fabric, and pin it in place. When you have finished pinning the lace on all sides and are back to where you started, cut the lace so that the ends overlap ½ inch.

5. Thread a needle, and make a beginning knot. Slide the needle between the lace and the fabric to hide the knot. With a small and even running stitch, sew the lace to the fabric, removing the pins as you sew. You will be sewing through the lace and the double-folded hem at the same time. Make an ending knot on the wrong side of the handkerchief.

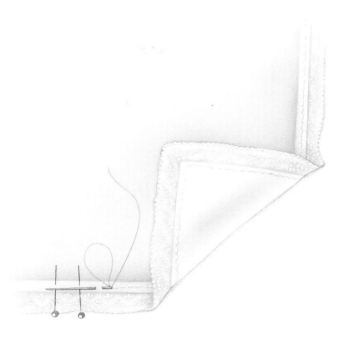

6. Hand wash the handkerchief in cool water with gentle soap. Hang to dry; then lightly press the handkerchief with an iron set on "cotton/steam."

Mary was braiding a new rug. She had cut worn-out woolen clothes in strips,
and Ma had put each color in a separate box. Mary kept the boxes in order and remembered
where each color was. She was braiding the rag-strips together in a long braid
that coiled down in a pile beside her chair. When she came to the end of a strip, she chose
the color she wanted and sewed it on. . . . Laura sewed the rag braid into a round rug
and laid it heavy over Mary's lap so that Mary could see it with her fingers.
THE LONG WINTER

 # Mary's Braided Rug

Although Mary lost her sight when the Ingalls family lived on Plum Creek, her blindness did not prevent her from working with her hands. All through the long winter, she braided and sewed strips of old fabric together to make a rug. Mary worked even when the storms made it so dark that Laura could not sew. "I can see with my fingers," Mary said.

You will need:

⅜ yard each of three calico fabrics
  (any small-patterned cotton)
needle (sharps)
thread
pins
4 clothespins
masking tape
scissors
ruler
pencil

1. With a ruler and a pencil, measure and mark two pieces, each measuring 2 x 45 inches, on each of your three fabrics. Cut out all six pieces on the marked lines.

2. On the wrong side of one 2-inch end of each piece, mark a sewing line ¼ inch from the edge.

3. Place the marked 2-inch ends of two matching pieces of fabric right sides together. Match the marked sewing lines, and pin. Thread a needle, and make a beginning knot. With a running stitch, sew along the sewing line. Make an ending knot, and remove the pins.

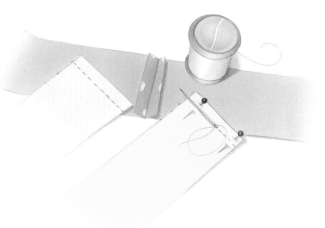

4. Repeat this step with the two other sets of matching fabric pieces. You now have three strips of fabric, each measuring about 2 x 90 inches.

5. Fold each fabric strip in half lengthwise, with the wrong sides touching each other. Use an iron set on "cotton/steam" to press the fold. Unfold the fabric, and lay it wrong side up on the ironing board. Fold both lengthwise edges toward the center crease until they touch at the crease. Press the folds with the iron. Place the two folded edges together lengthwise, fold along the

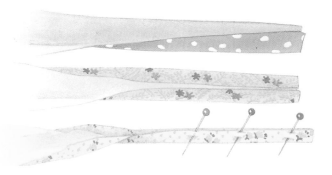

center crease, and pin every two inches along the entire length of the strip.

6. Hold the ends of the three fabric strips together with a clothespin. Thread a needle, and make a beginning knot. Take several stitches through the three ends to sew them together securely. Make an ending knot.

7. One at a time, wind the long end of each strip around your hand; this makes a bobbin. Take the bobbin off your hand, and hold each bobbin together with a clothespin. This will make it easier to braid the long ends.

8. Firmly tape the sewn end of your fabric strips to the back of a chair with masking tape. Braid the strips, removing the pins as you go along. Do not braid too tightly, or the braid will curl up at the edges. As you braid, release some of each fabric strip from its bobbin, then replace the clothespin.

When you finish braiding, put a clothespin on the end to keep the braid from unraveling. Remove the masking tape from the sewn end.

9. Thread a needle, and make a beginning knot. Curve the sewn end of the braid around to the side and then behind the braid. Whipstitch the end of the braid to the back of the braid. On a flat surface, coil the braid in a circle using masking tape to hold the coiled braid together. Continue to whipstitch the side edges of the braid together. As you sew, make sure the braid lies flat and the stitches aren't too tight, or the rug will buckle when you are finished. Coil and sew until you are one inch from the end of the shortest fabric strip.

10. Cut the remaining fabric ends even, and pin them to the back of the rug (the side you have been sewing on). Sew the ends to the rug with a whipstitch. Make an ending knot, and remove the pins.

When it is finished, your rug will be the perfect size for a doll's house, or for putting under a lamp, a plant, or a hot serving dish. You can make the rug smaller or larger by varying the width or changing the length of the fabric strips you use.

*Laura sat thinking. She was making a little picture frame
of cross-stitch in wools on thin, silver-colored cardboard. Up the sides and across
the top she had made a pattern of small blue flowers and green leaves.
Now she was outlining the picture-opening in blue. While she put the tiny needle
through the perforations in the cardboard and drew the fine, colored
wool carefully after it, she was thinking how wistfully Carrie had looked at the
beautiful thing. She decided to give it to Carrie for Christmas.
Someday, perhaps, she could make another for herself.*

THE LONG WINTER

Laura's Embroidered Picture Frame

When blizzard after blizzard forced the train across the prairie to stop running, all supplies were cut off for the families living in De Smet, South Dakota. Caught unprepared for Christmas, Laura decided to give Carrie a picture frame she had embroidered for herself. In May, when the train finally arrived with the Christmas barrel from Reverend Alden, it was full of wonderful gifts, including two boxes full of bright colored yarns, embroidery silks, and sheets of silver and gold perforated cardboard that Ma gave to Laura.

You will need:

*crewel wool or embroidery floss
   (blue, yellow, and green)
silver perforated paper (14 holes
   per inch)
needle (tapestry or embroidery)
small sharp-pointed scissors
glue*

*ruler
pencil
white poster board
needle threader
Picture Frame Embroidery Chart
   from the pattern pocket*

1. On the non-silver side of the perforated paper, use a pencil to mark a hole to be the starting point. Counting this hole as hole number 1, count 45 more holes across, and mark the ending point in hole number 46. With a ruler and a pencil, draw a line through the row of holes from hole number 1 to hole number 46. This line will measure about 3⅛ inches. Beginning at hole number 1, count 51 holes down, and use a pencil to place a mark in hole number 52. With a ruler and a pencil, draw a line that connects hole number 1 and hole number 52. This line will measure about 3½ inches. Repeat these directions to draw two more lines to form a rectangle, 46 holes across and 52 holes down. Cut out the rectangle on the marked lines. You how have a rectangle with 44 holes across and 50 holes down to stitch in.

2. Thread a needle with two strands of blue crewel yarn (or three strands of embroidery floss) 24 inches long. Pull the yarn through the eye of the needle, leaving one end longer than the other. Do not make a beginning knot.

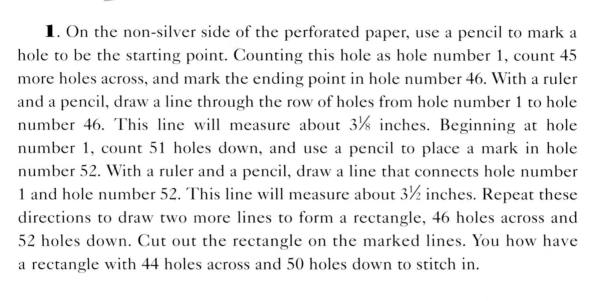

3. Find the Picture Frame Embroidery Chart in the pattern pocket, and cut it out. Begin at the upper left-hand corner of your perforated paper. Count four holes down and then seven holes across; this is your starting point. Push the needle up through this hole, leaving the thread end on the underside. Begin without a knot.

4. Sew with cross-stitches, following the Picture Frame Embroidery Chart. Each symbol on the chart represents a cross-stitch taken between four holes on the perforated paper. The different symbols represent different colors of floss or yarn as

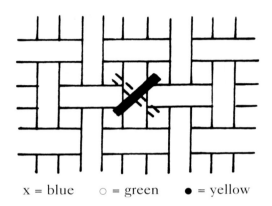

x = blue   o = green   ● = yellow

shown. Remember to take your first diagonal stitch of the cross-stitch from *bottom left* to *upper right*. The second diagonal stitch will cross over it from *bottom right* to *upper left*. Stitch all the blue flowers first, then the green leaves, and finally the yellow centers. This will save you from having to thread the needle several times for each flower. If you make a mistake, simply unthread the needle and pull out the incorrect stitch, using the blunt end of the needle. Thread the needle and start again.

5. Stitch the flowers around the frame clockwise. When you come to the end, or your thread is too short, end without a knot. If you need to continue stitching, thread more yarn or floss into the needle. Always begin and end without a knot.

6. Thread the needle with three strands of blue crewel yarn (or six strands of embroidery floss) 40 inches long. Pull the yarn through the eye of the

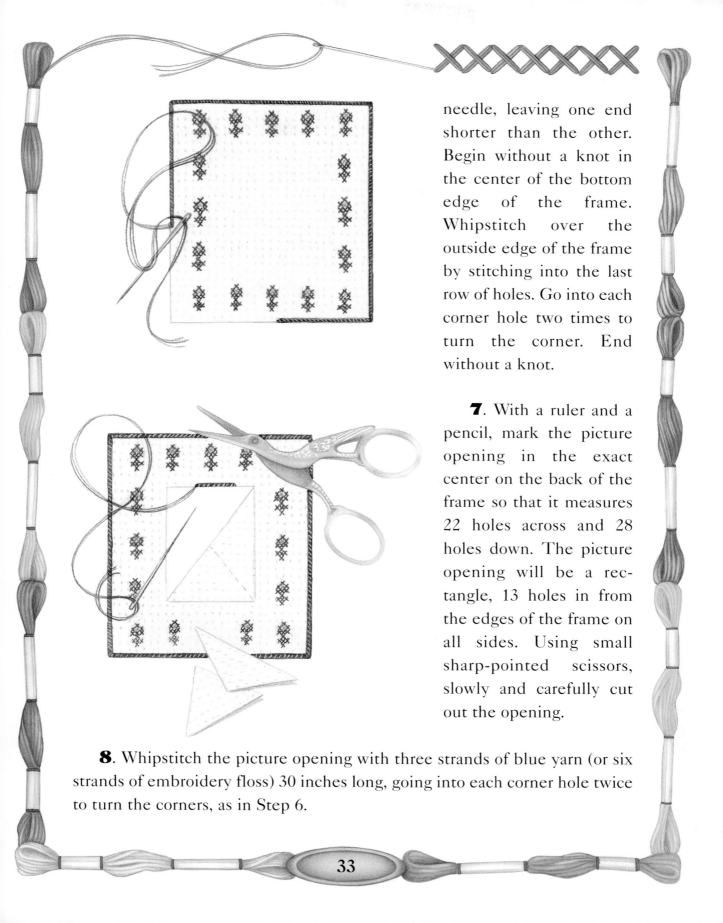

needle, leaving one end shorter than the other. Begin without a knot in the center of the bottom edge of the frame. Whipstitch over the outside edge of the frame by stitching into the last row of holes. Go into each corner hole two times to turn the corner. End without a knot.

7. With a ruler and a pencil, mark the picture opening in the exact center on the back of the frame so that it measures 22 holes across and 28 holes down. The picture opening will be a rectangle, 13 holes in from the edges of the frame on all sides. Using small sharp-pointed scissors, slowly and carefully cut out the opening.

8. Whipstitch the picture opening with three strands of blue yarn (or six strands of embroidery floss) 30 inches long, going into each corner hole twice to turn the corners, as in Step 6.

9. Cut four poster board pieces, each measuring $3\frac{1}{2}$ x $\frac{5}{8}$ inches. Glue two of these pieces together to make the support piece. Use a pencil and a ruler to mark a fold line on the support piece, $\frac{1}{2}$ inch from one short edge.

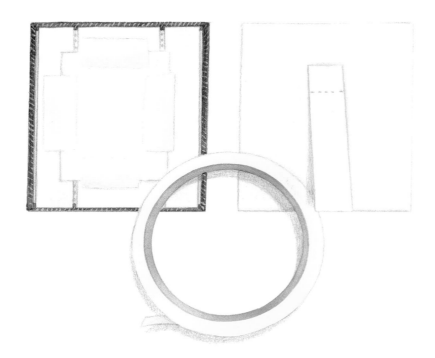

10. Glue the remaining two pieces to the long sides of the frame to cover the back of your stitching. Spread the glue thinly and evenly so that it doesn't show through the embroidery. Cut two pieces of poster board, each measuring $1\frac{1}{2}$ x $\frac{5}{8}$ inches, and glue these carefully to cover the short sides of the frame. Let it dry.

11. Center a picture or a photograph behind the opening, and tape it in place. Make sure it is centered properly before you glue on the back in the next step.

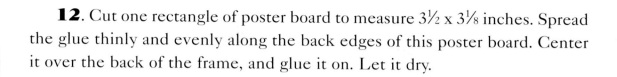

12. Cut one rectangle of poster board to measure 3½ x 3⅛ inches. Spread the glue thinly and evenly along the back edges of this poster board. Center it over the back of the frame, and glue it on. Let it dry.

13. Position your support piece on the back of the frame, so that the unmarked short end is even with the bottom of the frame. With a pencil, draw a line on the back of the frame to mark where you will glue the support piece. Bend the support piece on its marked line. Spread glue on the ½-inch section, and glue it in place on the back of the frame. Let the glue dry before you stand up your picture frame.

Mother knitted and rocked in her high-backed rocking-chair. Father carefully
scraped a new ax-handle with a bit of broken glass. Royal carved a chain of tiny links
from a smooth stick of pine, and Alice sat on her hassock, doing her woolwork
embroidery. And they all ate popcorn and apples, and drank sweet cider.

FARMER BOY

Alice's Embroidery Sampler

When beginning sewers used wool yarn to make an embroidery sampler, it was called woolwork embroidery. A sampler was made up of several different kinds of stitches. By making a sampler, a sewer was able to learn, practice, and remember these stitches. Almanzo's sister, Alice, entered her embroidery in a competition at the New York State Fair, where it won a first-prize blue ribbon.

You will need:

*12 x 14-inch piece of cotton or
    linenlike fabric
crewel wool or embroidery floss
    (dark red, light red, dark green,
    light green, or any other four
    colors)
transfer pencil
needle (embroidery)*

*scissors
embroidery hoop
needle threader
8 x 10-inch frame
masking tape or glue
Sampler Transfer Pattern from the
    pattern pocket*

1. Find the Sampler Transfer Pattern in the pattern pocket. The pattern is reversed, but once you transfer it to the fabric it will face the right way. With the transfer pencil, draw over all the stitching lines on the pattern. Once it has been drawn over with the transfer pencil, this transfer pattern can be used many times. Keep it in the pattern pocket.

2. Place the fabric, right side up, on an ironing board. Center the sampler pattern on the fabric so that the side you drew on with the transfer pencil touches the fabric. Heat an iron to the "cotton" setting. Place the hot iron on the paper pattern, and hold the iron in place for 10 to 15 seconds; then carefully slide it to another part of the pattern. Do not lift the iron off the pattern, and be careful not to shift the pattern. After you have held the iron on all parts of the pattern, lift up the edge of the paper pattern to see if the design has completely transferred to the fabric. Iron any section of the pattern again, if necessary. Hint: If the paper moves while you are ironing, the design might blur on the fabric. If this happens, follow the washing directions in Step 6; then try again.

3. Separate the two parts of the embroidery hoop, and lay the inner hoop on a flat surface. Lay the fabric over the hoop so that the house and hearts are within the ring. Press the outer hoop over the fabric, and adjust the screw until the fabric is stretched tight.

4. Begin your sampler by using cross-stitch to stitch the hearts. Thread a needle with one strand of light red crewel yarn (or two strands of embroidery floss) 20 inches long. Make a beginning knot. Push the needle up from underneath the fabric at the lower left of the first **X**, and stitch all the **X**'s by taking the first diagonal stitch of the cross-stitch from *bottom left* to *upper right*. The second diagonal stitch will cross over it from *bottom right* to *upper left*. To end off, push the needle through to the wrong side of the fabric. Make an ending knot by stitching under the backs of your embroidery stitches, not into the back of the fabric.

5. Follow the stitch instructions and diagrams on page 6, page 40, and page 41, and refer to the Stitch Guide on page 39 to finish the sampler. Stitch over all the transferred lines on your fabric. When your thread ends, or when you finish a section, make an ending knot as in Step 4. If you make a mistake, simply unthread the needle and pull out the incorrect stitch, using the blunt end of the needle. Thread the needle, and start again. As you finish each section within the hoop, move the hoop to a new part of the design.

6. When you have finished embroidering the sampler, hand wash it in cold water with gentle soap to remove the transfer pencil marks. Hang it to dry. Place the embroidered sampler, wrong side up, on an ironing board. Use an iron set on "cotton/steam" to press it flat and smooth.

7. Take apart the frame, and center the sampler over the cardboard backing. Fold the fabric edges over the cardboard, and secure the sampler by taping or gluing these edges to the cardboard. Place the sampler in the frame.

Stitch Guide

This is how your sampler will look after you transfer the pattern to your fabric. Follow the colors as shown, or choose your own colors.

running stitch

backstitch

A B C D E F G H I J K L M
N O P Q R S T U V W X Y Z

blanket stitch

cross-stitch

chain stitch

cross-stitch

1 2 3 4 5 6 7 8 9 0

herringbone stitch

lazy daisy stitch

cross-stitch

There are seven different kinds of stitches in this sampler. The back-stitch, the running stitch, and the cross-stitch are described in the Sewing Skills section on page 6. The other four stitches are described here. Follow the diagrams and instructions here and in the Sewing Skills section to learn each stitch. If you are left-handed, turn the book upside down so the diagrams are easy for you to follow. For best results, practice all the stitches on a piece of scrap fabric before you begin the sampler.

Beginning all embroidery stitches: Thread a needle, and make a beginning knot. Bring the needle up through the fabric at the beginning of the sewing line, and pull until the knot catches on the underside.

Chain stitch: Begin as above. Lay the thread over the stitching line, and hold the thread with the thumb of your other hand. Place the needle back into the fabric at the beginning of the sewing line, and push the needle tip forward along the underside of the fabric. At the beginning of the next chain stitch shown on your fabric, push the needle tip back up to the surface, and bring the needle over the thread held by your thumb. Pull the needle and thread slowly to form the first loop of the chain. Repeat to continue the chain, always pushing the needle into the fabric within the loop of the stitch you just made. To end off, put the needle tip into the fabric on the outside of the final loop to form a small stitch over the loop, and push the needle through to the underside. Make an ending knot by stitching under the backs of your embroidery stitches.

Lazy daisy stitch: Begin as above, bringing the needle up through the fabric at the center of the flower. This stitch is like chain stitch, but each new chain stitch is formed in a different direction. Follow the chain stitch directions to form one loop that covers one transferred petal on the fabric. To end each petal, push the needle tip into the fabric on the outside of the loop (forming a small stitch over the loop), and push the needle through to the underside. To make more petals on the daisy, always begin by bringing the needle up through the fabric at the center of the flower. End off the same as chain stitch.

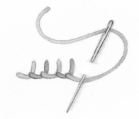

Blanket stitch: Begin as above, bringing the needle up through the fabric at the lower left of the blanket stitch line. * Hold the thread down on the surface of the fabric with the thumb of your other hand. Place the needle into the fabric at the top of the stitch. Push the needle tip along under the fabric, and bring the tip back to the surface where the stitching line bends, to form a corner. Pull the thread through the fabric and over the thread held by your thumb. Repeat from the * to cover the entire line of transferred stitches. To end off, put the needle tip into the fabric on the outside of the bend at the final corner, and push it through to the underside. Make an ending knot by stitching under the backs of your embroidery stitches.

Herringbone stitch: Begin as above, bringing the needle up through the fabric at the lower left of the herringbone stitch line. If you are left-handed, turn your sampler upside down. The first stitch slants up to the right. Follow the line up, and push the tip of the needle through the fabric at the end of it. Push the needle to the left along the underside of the fabric and then back through to the fabric surface at the top of the line that slants down to the right. Repeat this step, moving from the top to the bottom and then back to the top, always stitching from right to left. To end off, push the needle through to the underside at the end of the last stitching line. Make an ending knot by stitching under the backs of your embroidery stitches.

Carrie was playing on the bed and Laura and Mary
sat at the table. Mary was sorting quilt blocks and Laura was making a
little apron for the rag doll, Charlotte. The wind howled overhead
and whined in the stovepipe, but there was no snow yet.
ON THE BANKS OF PLUM CREEK

 # Laura's Doll Apron

Since they did laundry just once a week, Laura, Mary, and Ma each had to be very careful to keep their clothes clean. They wore aprons over their dresses every day, for the entire day. Laura made an apron for her doll, Charlotte, so that she could wear one, too.

You will need:

⅜ yard of plain cotton or calico fabric
½ yard of ⅜-inch grosgrain
   ribbon
thread
pencil

ruler
scissors
pins
needle (sharps)
glue stick

Making the Apron:

1. Find the Apron Pattern in the pattern pocket, and cut it out. Lay your fabric out on a flat surface, folding the fabric in half with the right sides touching each other to form two layers. Pin the Apron Pattern on the fabric layers.

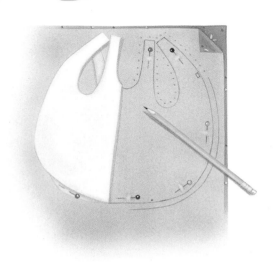

2. With a pencil, draw on the fabric around the edges of your pattern to make the sewing line. Draw marks on the fabric to match the circle marks on the pattern. Remove the pins holding the pattern; then pin the two layers of fabric together. With a ruler and a pencil, make marks about every inch, ¼ inch outside the sewing line, all around the apron. Connect these marks to make the cutting line.

3. Cut through both layers on the cutting line. With the layers still pinned together, turn the fabric pieces over and pin the pattern upside down to this unmarked side. Draw around the pattern to make the sewing line. Remove the pins and the pattern. You now have sewing lines on both pieces of fabric.

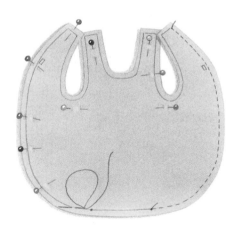

4. Match the sewing lines, and pin the apron pieces, right sides together. Place pins along all sewing lines. Thread a needle, and make a beginning knot. With a running stitch, sew on the sewing line from one shoulder edge to the circle mark on that side. Make an ending knot, and remove the pins from the seam. Repeat on the other side of the apron.

5. Thread a needle, and make a beginning knot. With a running stitch, sew from one shoulder edge to the other on the armhole sewing line. Make an ending knot. Repeat on the other armhole.

6. Thread a needle, and make a beginning knot. With a running stitch, sew from one shoulder edge to the other on the neck sewing line. Make an ending knot. Do not sew across the shoulder edges.

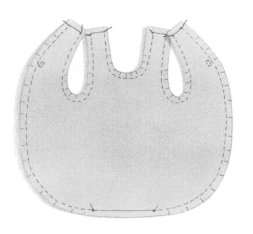

7. With scissors, clip the edge of the fabric in toward the sewing line along the curved edges. Do not cut through the sewing line. Turn the apron right side out through the bottom opening between the circle marks. Use a chopstick, knitting needle, or the eraser end of a pencil to push the seamed edges and the shoulder straps flat.

8. Fold both sides of the bottom opening on the sewing lines, so that the extra fabric is inside the opening. Pin the folded edges together. Use an iron set on "cotton/steam" to press the apron flat. Remove the pins. Use the glue stick to apply a small amount of glue to one edge of the fabric, inside the opening. Hold the edges together until the glue dries, to close the opening. Or, use a whipstitch to sew the folded edges together.

9. With a ruler and a pencil, draw a sewing line on the underside of the shoulder straps, ¼ inch from the shoulder edge. Match the sewing lines, and pin the right sides of each set of shoulder straps together. Thread a needle, and make a beginning knot. With a running stitch, sew one shoulder seam. Make an ending knot, and remove the pins. Repeat on the other shoulder seam.

10. Thread a needle, and make a beginning knot. Whipstitch the raw edges of one shoulder strap, to prevent fraying. Make an ending knot. Repeat on the other strap.

11. Cut the ribbon into two 9-inch pieces. Fold under ¼ inch on one end of the ribbon. Pin the folded side of the ribbon to the wrong side of the apron as shown on the pattern. Thread a needle, and make a beginning knot. Slide the needle between the ribbon and apron to hide the knot. With a running stitch, sew the ribbon to the apron, forming a rectangle of stitching as shown on the pattern. Make an ending knot, and remove the pins. Repeat on the other side with the other piece of ribbon.

Adding the pockets:

1. Find the Pocket Pattern in the pattern pocket, and cut it out. Lay the rest of your fabric on a flat surface, folding the fabric in half with the right sides touching each other, to form two layers. Pin the Pocket Pattern to the fabric layers.

2. With a pencil, draw on the fabric around the edges of your pattern to make the sewing line. Remove the pins holding the pattern; then pin the two layers of fabric together. With a ruler and a pencil, make marks about every inch, $\frac{1}{4}$ inch outside the sewing line, all around the pocket. Connect these marks to make the cutting line.

3. Cut through both layers on the cutting line. With the layers still pinned together, turn the pocket pieces over, and pin the pattern to this unmarked side. Draw around the pattern to make the sewing line. Remove the pins and the pattern. You now have sewing lines on both pieces of fabric.

4. Place one pocket piece, wrong side up, on an ironing board. Fold one side in on the sewing line. Use an iron set on "cotton/steam" to press the fold flat. Repeat on the other three sides. Fold the top pocket edge under on the fold line, and press it flat. Repeat on the other pocket.

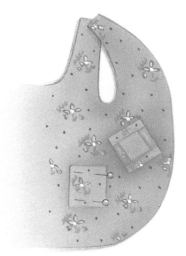

5. Pin both pockets, right side up, onto the right side of the apron as shown on the pattern. Thread a needle, and make a beginning knot. Starting underneath the upper corner of one pocket, push the needle up through the apron and pocket layers. With a running stitch, sew very close to the pocket edge down the side of the pocket, along the bottom, then up the other side. Leave the pocket open at the top. Push the needle through to the underside, and make an ending knot. Remove the pins. Repeat this step for the other pocket.

This apron will fit a 16- to 18-inch doll.

*The sun was so low now that each prairie swell began to
have its shadow lying eastward, and out of the large, pale sky the flocks of ducks and
the long wedges of geese were sliding down to Silver Lake to rest for the night.
The clean wind was blowing now with no dust in it, and Laura let her sunbonnet
slip down her back so that she could feel the wind on her face
and see the whole great prairie.*

BY THE SHORES OF SILVER LAKE

Laura's Prairie Sunbonnet

One autumn afternoon Pa took Laura to watch the men laying the railroad tracks near Silver Lake. Laura loved watching them work in rhythm to make the grade and lay the tracks in a straight line across the level prairie. Her sunbonnet's wide brim, which protected her skin from the harsh sun, also cut off her view of the world around her. So, as she often did, Laura let her bonnet hang by the ribbons down her back.

You will need:

*1 yard of calico fabric (any small-
  patterned cotton)
¼ yard of heavyweight nonwoven
  fusible interfacing (available at
  sewing supply stores)
27 inches of ⅝-inch-wide grosgrain
  ribbon
9 inches of ¼-inch-wide elastic
needle (sharps)
thread*

*ruler
pencil
pins
scissors
clear tape
safety pin
Sunbonnet Pattern and Sunbonnet
  Brim Patterns A and B from
  the pattern pocket*

Cutting out the pieces:

1. Find the Sunbonnet Brim Patterns A and B and the Sunbonnet Pattern in the pattern pocket, and cut them out. Match the two brim patterns along the joining lines, and tape them together to make one complete brim pattern.

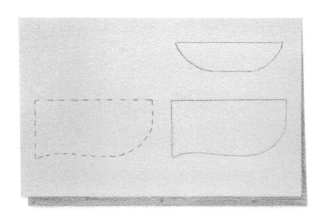

2. Lay your fabric out on a flat surface, folding the fabric in half to form two layers, with the right sides touching each other. Pin the Sunbonnet Pattern and Sunbonnet Brim Pattern on the fabric layers as shown in the layout guide. Be sure to leave enough fabric so that you can place and cut out the Sunbonnet Pattern again.

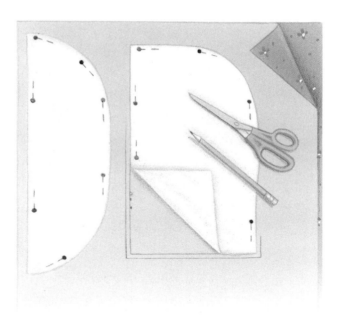

3. With a pencil, draw on the fabric around the edges of your patterns to make the sewing line. Draw square and circle marks on your fabric to match the marks on the pattern. Remove the patterns.

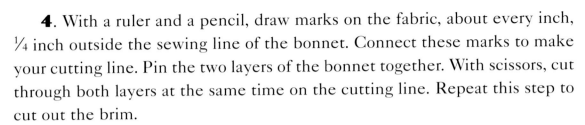

4. With a ruler and a pencil, draw marks on the fabric, about every inch, ¼ inch outside the sewing line of the bonnet. Connect these marks to make your cutting line. Pin the two layers of the bonnet together. With scissors, cut through both layers at the same time on the cutting line. Repeat this step to cut out the brim.

5. With the layers still pinned with the right sides together, turn the fabric pieces and the pattern pieces over. Pin the bonnet and brim patterns upside down to these unmarked wrong sides. Draw around each pattern to mark the sewing line. Draw the square and circle marks. Remove the patterns. You now have sewing lines on the wrong sides of both sides of the fabric.

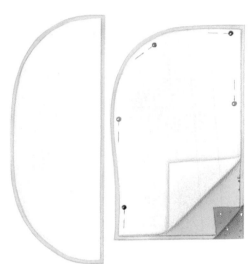

6. Use only the Sunbonnet Pattern to repeat Steps 2 through 5 on the rest of the layered fabric. You now have four bonnet pieces and two brims cut from the calico fabric. Set aside the four bonnet pieces.

Making the brim:

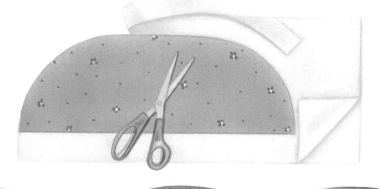

1. Lay out the fusible interfacing on a flat surface. Fold it in half to form two layers, with the shiny or bumpy sides together. Take one of your cut calico brim pieces and pin it, right side up, on the layered interfacing. Following the outside edge of the brim, cut the interfacing to make two interfacing brims. Unpin the calico.

2. Place one calico brim piece, wrong side up, on an ironing board. Use an iron set on "cotton/steam" to press the brim smooth. Darken the brim sewing lines with a pencil, so that you will be able to see them through the interfacing later. Carefully place the shiny or bumpy side of one interfacing brim on the wrong side of the calico brim, with the outside edges even. The fusing glue on the shiny or bumpy side of the interfacing will make the fabric and the interfacing stick together.

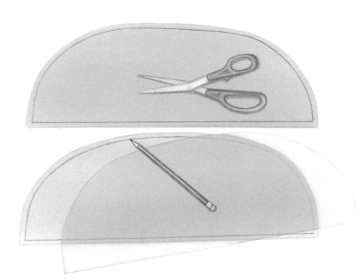

3. With the iron still set on "cotton/steam," fuse the fabric to the interfacing by placing the iron on the interfacing. Hold the iron in one place for 10 seconds; then carefully move the iron to another area. Repeat until the entire brim has been fused. Set this fused brim aside. Now repeat Steps 2 and 3 with the other calico brim and interfacing brim pieces.

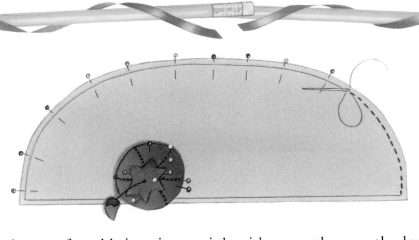

4. Pin the two fused brim pieces, right sides together, on the long curved edge, matching the sewing lines that show through the interfacing. Thread a needle, and make a beginning knot. With a running stitch, sew this curved seam, stitching through the layers of the fabric and the interfacing. Do not sew the seam on the straight edge. Make an ending knot. Remove the pins.

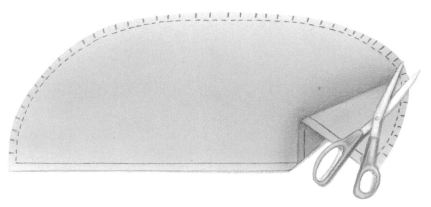

5. With scissors, clip the edge of the fabric toward the curved edge seam. Do not cut through the sewing line. Turn the brim right side out. Use an iron set on "cotton/steam" to press the curved edge smooth and flat. Set the brim aside.

Making the bonnet:

1. Pin the right sides of two of the four bonnet pieces together, matching the sewing lines along the back curved edge. Thread a needle, and make a beginning knot. With a running stitch, sew the back curved seam. Make an ending knot, and remove the pins. Repeat with the other two bonnet pieces. You have joined the four pieces to make the inside and the outside of the bonnet.

2. With scissors, clip the edges of the fabric toward both of the curved edge seams. Do not cut through the sewing lines. Open up each bonnet piece to the right side and place this side down. Keeping the edges of each curved seam 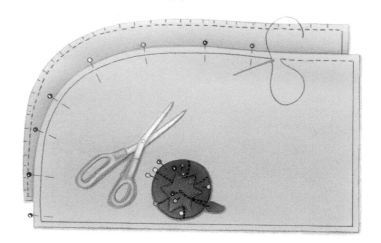 together, press them flat, away from each seam, with an iron set on "cotton/steam." Do not open the seams.

3. With each bonnet open to the right side, place the bonnets together, with the right sides touching. Match the circle and square marks. Pin the inside and the outside of the bonnet together along the lower edge between the square marks.

4. Thread a needle, and make a beginning knot. With a running stitch, sew the short distance between one square and the first circle mark. Make an ending knot. Leave an opening between the circles. Make a beginning knot,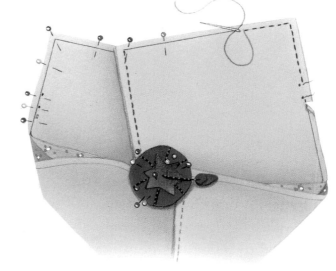

and begin sewing at the second circle. Sew to the lower circle on the other side of the bonnet. Make an ending knot. Leave an opening between the circles. Make a beginning knot, and sew from the upper circle to the square mark. Make an ending knot, and remove the pins.

5. With scissors, clip the edge of the fabric to each square mark.

6. Turn the bonnet right side out. Use a chopstick, knitting needle, or the eraser end of a pencil to push out the corners. Use an iron set on "cotton/steam" to press the corners and the seam flat.

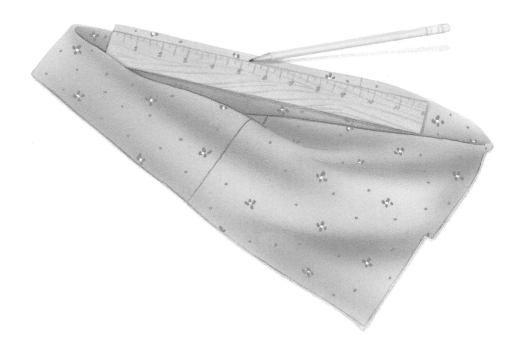

7. Lay the bonnet on a flat surface. The front edge sewing lines are already marked on the wrong side of both the inside and the outside of the bonnet. With a ruler and a pencil, also draw front edge sewing lines on the *right sides* of both bonnets between the clips at the two square marks.

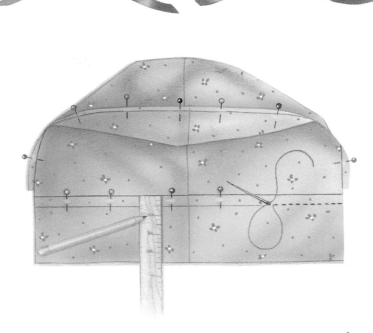

8. With the ruler and pencil, draw another sewing line 2½ inches from the bottom edge, on the right side of the fabric. Draw a second line ½ inch above the first line, in the position shown on the Sunbonnet Pattern. Make sure that these sewing lines are parallel to the bottom edge and that the openings in the side seams are between them. Pin both sides of the bonnet together along the parallel sewing lines.

9. Thread a needle, and make a beginning knot. Hide the knot between both sides of the bonnet, and sew with a running stitch from one edge to the other on the top parallel sewing line. Make an ending knot. Repeat on the bottom line. Remove the pins. You have now made the bonnet.

Attaching the bonnet to the brim:

1. With the wrong sides of the bonnet together, match the center seams and the front edge sewing lines between the clips at the square marks. Pin the two layers together. Cut a piece of thread 30 inches long. Thread a needle, and make a beginning knot. Push the needle through the fabric at one square mark. Take one back-stitch to secure the knot. With a running stitch, sew through both layers on the front edge sewing line to the other square mark. Do *not* make an ending knot or cut the thread. Pull the

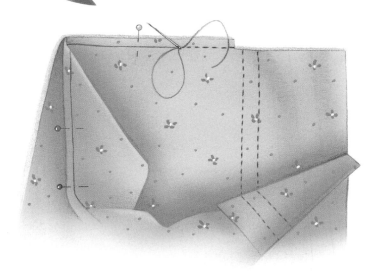

thread from the needle, and leave it long. This row of running stitches is your gathering thread.

2. The straight edge of one layer of the brim will now be pinned to the bonnet; the other layer is not attached now. Match one side edge of the brim to the bonnet at the square mark where the gathering thread begins, and pin. Match the other side edge of the brim to the square mark where the gathering thread ends, and pin. Fold the brim in half to find the center of the straight edge, match the center to the bonnet center seam, and pin. Be careful to pin the bonnet edge to only one layer of the brim.

3. The bonnet edge is much larger than the brim edge. Pull the loose end of the gathering thread to gather the bonnet edge until it is the same length as the brim edge. Wrap the gathering thread around the end pin, to keep the gathers in place. Adjust the gathers so they are evenly spaced along the brim edge.

4. Start at the beginning knot of the gathering thread, and place a pin every ½ inch to hold the gathered bonnet edge to one layer of the smooth brim edge. Make sure the gathers are evenly spaced between the pins.

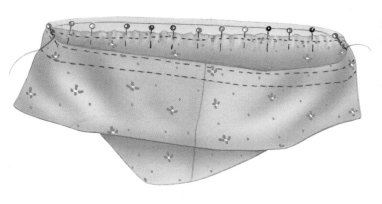

5. Thread a needle, and make a beginning knot. The gathering thread is already on the sewing line. With a running stitch, sew another line of stitches over the gathering thread on the sewing line, between the square marks. Make sure you sew only one layer of the brim to the bonnet edge, as the other layer will be attached later. When you come to the end of the sewing line, make an ending knot and remove the pins.

6. Fold the edge of the unattached layer of the brim under on the sewing line. Use an iron set on "cotton/steam" to press it flat. Press the gathered bonnet seam edges toward the brim. Place the fold of the unattached brim edge over the gathered seam edges to cover them. Pin the folded edge of the brim along the bonnet-brim seam line.

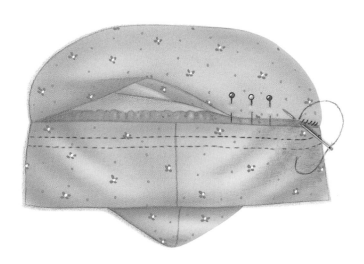

7. Thread a needle, and make a beginning knot. Whipstitch the folded edge of the brim to the gathers along the bonnet-brim seam, so the seam is covered. Make an ending knot, and remove the pins.

Attaching the ribbons:

1. Cut the 27-inch ribbon in half. Fold one end of the ribbon under, and pin it to one end of the elastic. Thread a needle, and make an ending knot. Sew the ribbon to the elastic with several running stitches. Make an ending knot, and remove the pins. Repeat this step to sew the remaining ribbon to the other end of the elastic. Pin the safety pin to one end of the ribbon-elastic strip.

2. Push the safety pin into the seam opening on one side edge of the bonnet. Inch the pin between the parallel stitching lines by gathering the bonnet over the pin and then moving the pin forward. If the pin gets caught at the center seam, keep trying until you can push past it. Bring the pin out through the seam opening on the other side. Pull the ribbon until just the elastic is inside the bonnet, and a ribbon is on each bonnet side. Remove the safety pin.

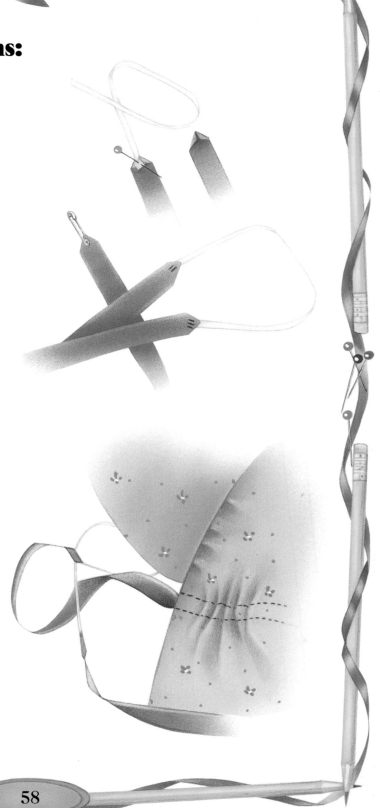

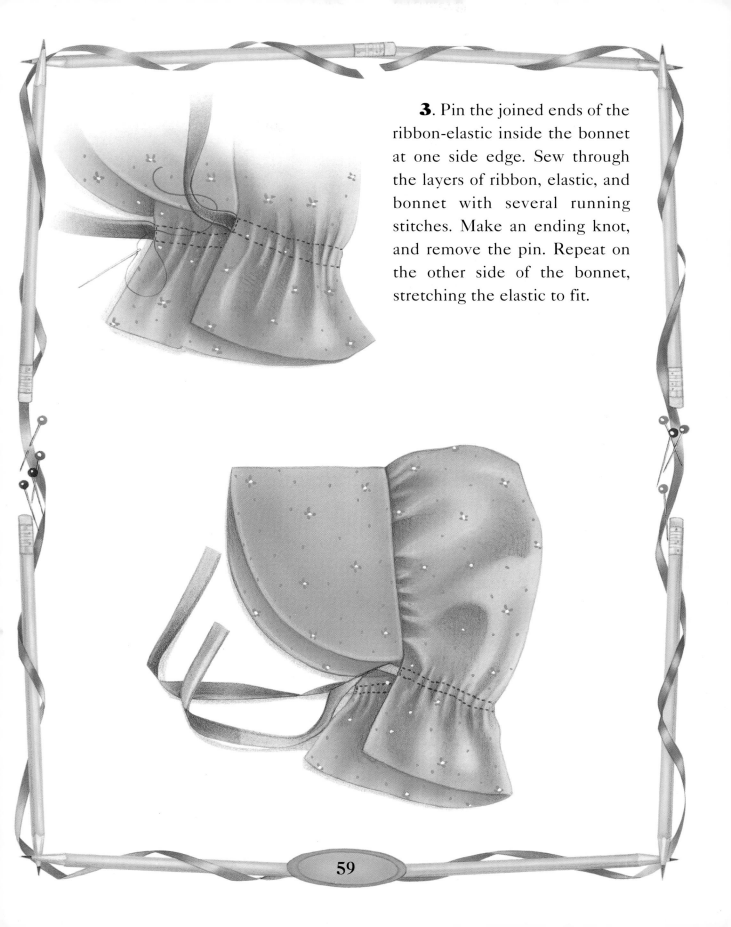

3. Pin the joined ends of the ribbon-elastic inside the bonnet at one side edge. Sew through the layers of ribbon, elastic, and bonnet with several running stitches. Make an ending knot, and remove the pin. Repeat on the other side of the bonnet, stretching the elastic to fit.

Index